THE SHABBY TABBY

by

Mardi Edwards

The contents of this work, including, but not limited to, the accuracy of events, people, and places depicted; opinions expressed; permission to use previously published materials included; and any advice given or actions advocated are solely the responsibility of the author, who assumes all liability for said work and indemnifies the publisher against any claims stemming from publication of the work.

All Rights Reserved
Copyright © 2024 by Mardi Edwards

No part of this book may be reproduced or transmitted, downloaded, distributed, reverse engineered, or stored in or introduced into any information storage and retrieval system, in any form or by any means, including photocopying and recording, whether electronic or mechanical, now known or hereinafter invented without permission in writing from the publisher.

Dorrance Publishing Co
585 Alpha Drive
Suite 103
Pittsburgh, PA 15238
Visit our website at www.dorrancebookstore.com

ISBN: 979-8-88729-135-2
eISBN: 979-8-88729-635-7

Stop! Stop! Come back for me! Meow! Meow! Shabby Tabby's cries were too small to hear.

The little shabby tabby shivered in the street. *Why did my family leave me alone, cold, and hungry?*

Meow! She took shelter in a big bush in front of the school.

Grrr...! That's my belly. She fought back the hunger by licking her paws and fell asleep for the night.

Shabby Tabby woke to the hustle and bustle of children getting off school buses. She spied the open doors of the school, leaped from the bush, and raced to the door. In the crowd, one girl lifted the shabby tabby in her arms.

This girl's arms are warm, but I smell food. Meow! She jumped away.

The little girl shouted, "Catch that cat!"

But Shabby Tabby was too fast for the girl.

The cat ran down the hallway into a big kitchen. She snuck in and quickly grabbed a piece of bacon from a plate on the counter. *Meow! Bacon! Bacon!*

"Hey," yelled the cook. "Where did you come from? Shoo! Get out of here."

The shabby tabby ran into a classroom, crawled under a desk, and gobbled up the bacon.

"A cat! A cat!" yelled the children.

"Where?" asked Mrs. Edwards, the teacher.

Shabby Tabby pounced from desk to desk and raced around the room. *Meow! Where is the door?*

Mrs. Edwards closed the door and bent down.

Meow! Are you nice?

"Don't be afraid. I won't hurt you," Mrs. Edwards said.

Shabby Tabby nudged against the teacher's leg. *Meow! Purr… Purr!*

Another little girl petted Shabby Tabby and held her close. "She is shaking."

These little girl's arms feel so good... Nap time!

"Can we keep her?" the little girl asked.

"I don't know. Let's ask our principal!" said Mrs. Edwards. She called the principal on the classroom phone. "Please come to see our new visitor."

In a few minutes, Mrs. Napier, the principal, walked into the classroom, and pointed to Shabby Tabby. "That's the cat I saw earlier outside in the cold."

"Can we keep her?" a little girl asked.

"Can we keep her?" a little boy asked.

Mrs. Napier put a finger to her lip. "Shh!" Mrs. Napier said. "Too late, you woke her."

Shabby Tabby jumped out of the girl's arms and pranced over to rub against the principal's leg. *"Meow! Purr... Purr...! Please like me!"*

Mrs. Napier bent down to pet the cat. "We can't have a cat at school. Some children are allergic to cats. Who would take care of her? Why would we keep a cat at school?"

"A mouse! A mouse!" screamed Mrs. Edwards. Mrs. Napier jumped up on a chair.

Shabby Tabby chased the mouse and caught it. *Easy catch! Look what I can do!*

"Yeah!" Everyone cheered.

"Is it alive?" Mrs. Edwards whispered. "We have been seeing mice in our room all week. They come in to get warm."

Mrs. Napier stepped down from the chair. "Maybe we do need a cat in the school," she said. "Then the mice will stay out."

Everyone watched Shabby Tabby.

GULP!

"Meow! Purr... Purr!" I think I have found a new home!

THE END